Text copyright © 2000 Anthony Masters
Illustrations copyright © 2000 Andrew Skilleter
Volume copyright © 2000 Hodder Wayland

Series concept: Wendy Knowles

Published in Great Britain in 2000 by Hodder Wayland,
an imprint of Hodder Children's Books

A catalogue record for this book is available from the British Library.

ISBN 0 7500 2958 7

Printed in Hong Kong by Wing King Tong Company Limited.

Hodder Children's Books
A division of Hodder Headline Limited
338 Euston Road, London NW1 3BH

IN SEARCH OF THE
BOY KING

Anthony Masters

Illustrated by
Andrew Skilleter

an imprint of Hodder Children's Books

Introduction –
The Valley of the Kings

The tombs in the Valley of the Kings were
built between 1552–1085 BC in the period of
Egyptian history which was called the New
Kingdom. The bodies of the dead pharaohs,
the rulers of the Egyptian people, were buried
in these rocky tombs in a remote valley in
an attempt to keep them safe from robbers.
In the past, the Egyptians had buried their
kings in pyramids, but these were easily
broken into.

The tombs were full of valuables. The
pharaohs were buried with many of their
personal belongings, their bodies embalmed
as mummies in surroundings that were made
as beautiful as possible. No expense was
spared, and the coffins and walls of the tombs
were often covered in precious jewels.

The Egyptian people loved life but they
believed that death would be an even better
experience for their kings. That is why the
kings would need their favourite belongings
around them.

They also believed that the survival of the dead person's spirit would depend on how well the body was looked after in the tomb.

The workmen who built the tombs in the Valley of the Kings lived in a special village nearby called Deir-el Medina. They were craftsmen who passed on their skills from father to son, and they had instructions to make the tombs as magnificent as possible, using the most valuable materials.

Because there was so much treasure to steal, thieves often broke into the tombs. Many of the tombs were found to have curses written on the walls. They were probably put there to frighten off would-be robbers. A strange series of deaths did in fact occur to some of those who entered the tombs.

Today, the Valley of the Kings is still being explored, although much of the treasure has been removed and displayed in museums. Studying the tombs is very important, as they present a fascinating record of life and religion in Ancient Egypt.

Chapter 1

"Wait," said Ahmed's father. "I think I know where the boy king's tomb might be."

Ahmed gazed at him in amazement. Over the years there had been so many digs in the Valley of the Kings, but the young pharaoh Tutankhamun's tomb had never been found. "Where?" Ahmed asked. "There's nowhere else left to look."

"Come and see." His father led the way across the valley. It was so hot and a dusty haze covered the boiling midday sun.

"What's so special about this spot?" Ahmed asked. "We didn't find anything here, did we? Except the ruins of those old huts."

"That's the point," said his father, gripping Ahmed's arm. "Those huts were lived in thousands of years ago by workers like us – but they were decorating Ramesses VI's tomb – not looking for the boy king. I think the huts could have been built over the entrance to another tomb."

"What makes you think that?"

"I found a step cut in the rock and I think there might be more."

"Why didn't we find them before?"
Ahmed was full of questions.

"They were covered in sand." His
father was very excited. "Why don't
you go and tell Mr Carter?"

Ahmed paused. He'd always been scared of the Englishman who was in charge of the excavation to find Tutankhamun's tomb. Howard Carter had been impatient recently because the dig seemed to be a failure.

"He won't be angry," laughed Ahmed's father. "He'll be delighted. It would be good for a young boy to break the news. After all, you're not much older than Tutankhamun when he was crowned."

Chapter 2

Ahmed ran over the sand as fast as he could, the dust flying up into his nose, ears and mouth. He was sweating with excitement. The boy king was the most mysterious person in the history of the Valley of the Kings. No one knew much about him, except that he was royal and had reigned for only a very short time.

Ahmed finally reached Howard Carter's tent, but at first one of Carter's servants came out and tried to push him away. "Mr Carter is a busy man. He doesn't want to see boys."

"He wants to see Tutankhamun, doesn't he?" yelled Ahmed.

Grumbling, the servant went back inside the tent, but Carter was already coming out, tall and commanding.

Ahmed shivered. "We – I – my father and his men—"

"Spit it out, boy," snapped Carter. "Or have you come to make a joke? If so—"

Eventually Ahmed persuaded Carter that he wasn't joking. Howard Carter could still hardly believe his good luck. By the end of the afternoon sixteen shallow steps had been revealed.

"I've waited so long for this," muttered Carter and then turned to Ahmed in delight. "This is fantastic! Will you come and work alongside me?"

"But it was my father who found the step," pointed out Ahmed.

"And you were the messenger," said Carter. "You brought the good news."

"I'd love to come and help you, Mr Carter," Ahmed replied, hardly able to catch his breath.

Chapter 3

By the following afternoon the
excavations had revealed a flight of
steps and the top of a muddy doorway.
On it was the seal of the ancient
Necropolis Guard – a group of priests
whose job it was to keep out robbers
and make sure the ancient tombs and
their treasures were kept safe inside.

In his excitement, on November 6th, 1922, Carter sent Lord Carnarvon, who had paid for the dig, a cable which read:

AT LAST HAVE MADE WONDERFUL
DISCOVERY IN THE VALLEY;
A MAGNIFICENT TOMB WITH SEALS
INTACT; AWAITING YOUR ARRIVAL.
CONGRATULATIONS.

But Ahmed thought that Carter was being too hopeful. He had noticed that the door of the tomb had been broken open – and then closed up again. This meant that robbers could have stolen the treasure.

Some days later, Ahmed and his
friend, Iqbal, were helping to clear
the doorway. When the stonework was
eventually removed they gazed down a
long sloping corridor filled with rubble.
But in one corner, a narrow passage
had been cut through.

Ahmed looked up at Howard Carter and wondered if they were both thinking the same thing. Thieves had definitely entered the tomb. When the rubble was finally cleared, they reached another door which had also been broken open and closed again.

"We're not going to find anything," Carter muttered to Ahmed. "I bet the treasure was all cleared out years ago."

In a strange way, Carter and Ahmed had struck up a passing friendship and Ahmed wondered if he saw him as a lucky companion.

With trembling hands, Carter made a tiny hole in the top left-hand corner of the door. He then began a series of tests to make sure that there were no poisonous gases in the chamber beyond.

Eventually, Carter inserted a candle into the hole in the door. Escaping hot air made the flame flicker but at least it didn't go out. This was a good sign.

If there were any poisonous gases inside, the flame would have gone out immediately. Then Carter stared through the hole – and kept on gazing into the chamber.

"What can you see?" asked Lord Carnarvon, who had just arrived, unable to bear the suspense any longer.

"I can see… *wonderful things*," whispered Carter.

Chapter 4

Later, Ahmed followed Carter and
Carnarvon and the other members of
the dig into the chamber. Although it
had obviously been ransacked by
thieves, they seemed to have been
interrupted, leaving the guards to
replace the treasures wherever they
could find space.

Ahmed could see clothes that must have been over 3,000 years old bundled into boxes just like rags, while furniture and vases, all priceless antiques, had been thrown on top of each other and heaped up anywhere.

"What a mess," said Carter.

"But what a discovery," Lord Carnarvon reminded him.

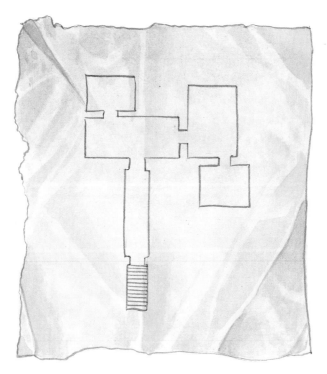

Who was Tutankhamun? And why did he become a king? But, most importantly, why did he die so young? Ahmed wondered. Maybe he would find out all the answers if he stuck close to Carter.

Ahmed and his father and the other workers carefully began to examine the treasure. They found three gilded wooden beds with carved animal heads, bows and arrows, and walking sticks. Then, under one of the beds, Ahmed found a long decorated box that contained a trumpet. A few minutes later he found some flowers. Ahmed stared at them in amazement. They looked just as if they had been freshly picked. Had they all been tricked? Obviously someone must have got there first.

Then Howard Carter came over to him, smiling. "I know what you're thinking, Ahmed," he said.

"Someone got here before us?" Ahmed asked.

"No, they didn't. The tomb was sealed – and after the break-in it was quickly sealed again. There would have been little or no air getting into the chamber. It's like being suspended in time. Even if the flowers were placed here on the day of the boy king's funeral, they would have stayed as fresh as when they were picked."

Ahmed gazed at the flowers again. "That means they're more than three thousand years old!"

"Something like that," said Carter, moving away to discover more treasure, this time a couple of golden chariots and, to the right of them, two black and gold life-size statues standing guard outside a plastered wall.

Then, under another of the beds, a low doorway could be seen.

Chapter 5

"Come on, Ahmed," said Carter. "You can squeeze under there. I want you to tell me what's through that doorway."

Ahmed managed to get under the bed and, armed with Carter's torch, pulled himself towards a second, smaller chamber. "What can you see?" asked Carter urgently.

"It's another chamber. Much smaller than this one."

Ahmed scanned the room with his torch. "But it's even more crowded with objects."

"Tell me what they are," Carter urged him, barely able to contain himself.

"More beds, chairs and boards – the kind you use to play games on."

"What are they made of?"

"Ivory – and gold, I think."

"Well done, Ahmed. Now get yourself out of there."

When he finally crawled back, his father whispered, "You've definitely become Carter's friend."

"More than that," said Iqbal, who had overheard. "I'm sure Mr Carter thinks you bring him good luck."

"I've got to see Tutankhamun," said Ahmed. "I have to know what he looked like."

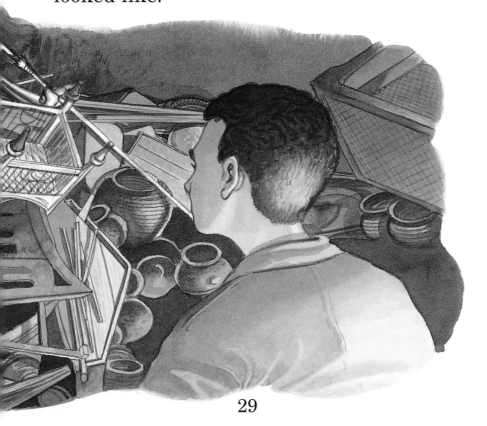

Chapter 6

Ahmed had to wait for over four years
before the boy king's mummy was at last
revealed. The dig took a long time to
finish. The nearby tomb of Seti II was
turned into a laboratory and storehouse
for the precious objects that were taken
out of Tutankhamun's tomb. Ahmed
continued to work for Howard Carter
and in the spring of 1923 Carter said
they were all 'in for a surprise' and that
he had discovered 'another wonder'.

Ahmed helped Carter to chip away at some of the plastered wall. Then, an astonishing sight was revealed. Behind the plaster was what appeared to be a wall of solid gold. Soon, however, Carter realized that the wall was really a series of four shrines, nesting one inside the other and covered with heavy gold leaf.

So huge was the block of shrines that only a small passage lay between it and the outer walls. When Ahmed and Iqbal squeezed through, they found that the walls were painted with scenes from the young king's life and also showed his journey through death into re-birth as one of the gods.

To the right there was an open doorway into another small room, but there was a shadow at the entrance. "What's the matter?" asked Carter. Ahmed and Iqbal froze. The shadow looked like a crouched guard dog, ready to spring. Carter pushed past the boys to look. "That's Anubis," he said. "He can't hurt you."

Ahmed and Iqbal moved on, past the statue with a wild dog's head. It was incredibly life-like. "Who was Anubis?" asked Ahmed.

"A god who watched over and protected the dead," replied Carter, leading the way into the room and gasping with amazement.

Here the treasures were even greater.

Chapter 7

The examination of the shrines was to take a very long time and it was not until October 1926 that the boy king was finally uncovered. By that time Ahmed had become a man.

Each of the four shrines was different, and between them more treasure was found. When the last shrine was removed, Ahmed was desperate to know what was inside the yellow quartz tomb. It had a lid of pink granite, painted to match the base, and was cracked from side to side.

Carter regularly invited audiences to watch the dramatic unfolding of the dig and this was the high point. The boy king himself was about to be uncovered. Ahmed could hardly bear to watch as the coffin lid was raised. Suppose it was empty?

Carter slowly lifted the lid. At first Ahmed and the others gathered around were bitterly disappointed for all they could see were linen shrouds. But, as the last shroud was lifted, Ahmed and every member of the audience gasped in wonder and amazement. A golden effigy of the boy king, Tutankhamun, lay there in all its magnificent glory.

Later, Ahmed helped to attach ropes to the silver handles of the coffin. Once the first coffin was pulled out, its lid was lifted to reveal a second on which had been placed a tiny wreath of blue lotus and cornflowers.

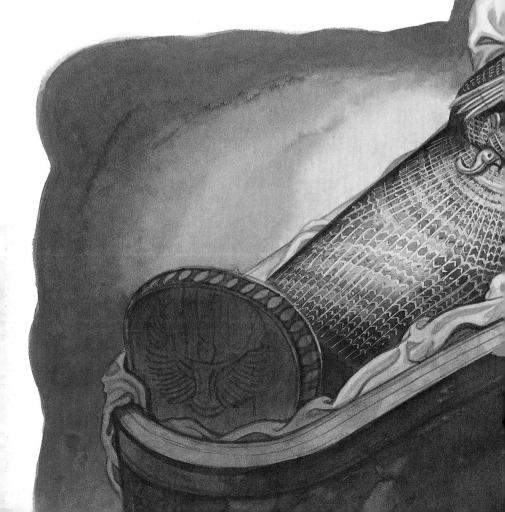

On October 17th, 1926, the second coffin lid was opened to reveal a third that was made of solid gold. No wonder it had all been so heavy.

"We're at the end," said Carter, glancing at Ahmed sadly.

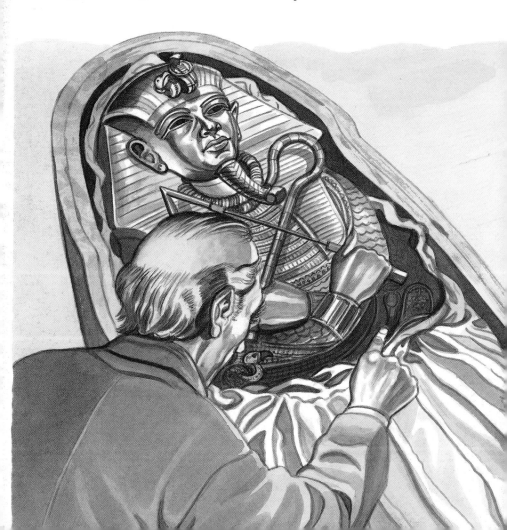

Then Carter opened the lid of the third and final coffin. Tutankhamun's mummy lay there, a golden mask covering his face. His body had been badly damaged by ointments and only the face, protected by the mask, had survived.

A few weeks later, Ahmed saw Carter walking across the valley and ran up to him.

"How old was Tutankhamun when he died?" Ahmed asked.

"About eighteen."

"How did he die?"

"I'm not sure."

"Who was he?"

Carter paused. "I think he was the son of Akhenaten. He was a very powerful king who rejected all the other gods and worshipped only the sun."

After that conversation Ahmed never saw Howard Carter again.

Chapter 8

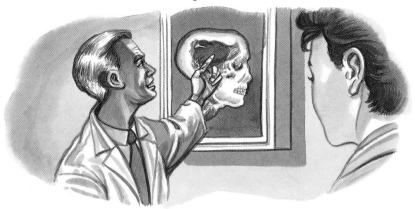

Many years later, an X-ray proved that
Tutankhamun had been murdered,
probably by a blow to the head. Ahmed
often dreamt of the boy king and
wondered if the tomb, like so many in
the Valley of the Kings, had been
cursed. It was certainly a strange
coincidence that Georges Bénédite,
Head of the Department of Egyptian
Antiquities at the Louvre in Paris,
died of a stroke after leaving the tomb.
Soon after that, Arthur C. Mace, an
expert from the Metropolitan Museum
of Art in New York, also died.

Shocked at these deaths people began to remember inscriptions that had been found in other tombs, warning that 'the lives of those who come to violate the tombs' would meet with a violent end. But although Lord Carnarvon died young, he had never really recovered from a road accident, and Howard Carter himself lived until 1939.

For a while, Ahmed was deeply afraid that he, too, would be cursed. But nothing happened and he continued to work in the Valley of the Kings for many years.

Ahmed felt strangely close to the murdered boy king for the rest of his life.

Glossary

afterlife the spiritual life after death.

antiquities objects from ancient times.

archaeologist someone who specializes in finding and identifying objects from ancient times.

cable a message given by phone and delivered by a messenger in person.

dig a site where archaeologists are hoping to make a discovery.

effigy a statue, or likeness.

excavation another word for a dig (see above).

gilded covered with gold or a gold-colour substance.

granite a hard rock used for building.

ivory a hard white substance from the tusk of an elephant.

linen a type of cloth.

priceless more valuable than can be
   expressed in money.

quartz a hard rock.

ransack to search a place thoroughly, often
   leaving it in a mess and stealing items.

seal a piece of wax attached to an object and
   stamped with an official picture to confirm
   that it has not been opened.

shrine a chest holding something sacred.

shroud a large piece of cloth, wrapped round
   a dead body in Egyptian times.

tomb a large underground chamber for the
   burial of the dead.

wreath a woven circle of flowers often put
   on a grave.